HE GIVES US SIGNS

HE GIVES US SIGNS

Gerald Coates

HODDER AND STOUGHTON
LONDON SYDNEY AUCKLAND TORONTO

British Library Cataloguing in Publication Data

Coates, Gerald
    He gives us signs.—(Foundations).—
    (Hodder Christian paperbacks).
    1. Christian life
    I. Title   II. Series
    248.4   BV4501.2

    ISBN 0-340-41073-6

CONTENTS

To all pioneers, in every area of the kingdom of God, who are willing to take a chance: Be the first – and make it happen!

FAITH-BUILDERS FOR THE FAITHFUL

If the Spirit of Him who raised Jesus from the dead dwells in you, He who raised Christ Jesus from the dead will also give life to your mortal bodies through His Spirit who indwells you (Romans 8:11 NASB)

Yet the body is not for immorality, but for the Lord; and the Lord is for the body . . . Or do you not know that your body is a temple of the Holy Spirit who is in you, whom you have from God, and that you are not your own? For you have been bought with a price: therefore glorify God in your body (1 Corinthians 6:13, 19–20 NASB)

And the very God of peace sanctify you wholly; and I pray God your whole spirit and soul and body be preserved blameless unto the coming of our Lord Jesus Christ (1 Thessalonians 5:23 AV)

We know that in all things God works for good with those who love him, those whom he has called according to his purpose (Romans 8:28 GNB)

INTRODUCTION

A different route

I have not always believed what I have written in this book.

I say that because we tend to categorise people quickly. This is not always bad. Sometimes it enables us to read people's writings with great interest. But often it deters us from different perspectives because we have put people into pigeonholes, labelling them 'good' or 'bad', 'acceptable' or 'unacceptable'.

When we hear someone speaking publicly we find it very easy to assume, 'That person's always been like this.' Invariably, though, it is an inaccurate assessment. Most of us have come through traumatic and painful periods, with dramatic changes in our philosophy, theology and outlook as well as our relationships. Many of these changes occur only after a great deal of personal heartache. Indeed to gain the most from a 'new experience' one occasionally has to deny a previous one.

My background was Anglican. I was far too young then to have coordinated my beliefs and approach to scripture and church life. Later on, when I experienced personal conversion, I joined the Plymouth Brethren. I am grateful for much of what they taught me. However, my Assembly relegated signs and wonders and healings to a period that existed two thousand years ago, four thousand miles away from Britain.

After several years I asked myself in utter frustration, 'Surely there must be more to the church than this?' Thank God there was. So began my long and painful route towards what I now believe to be a more appropriate perspective in this whole area.

Join in the journey

Stay with me as I take you through and past wrongly held beliefs, poorly thought-out theological positions, defensive postures, and – of late – wildly exaggerated claims and counterclaims.

Miracles and healings (both real and supposed) are the stuff that makes the dust swirl, heads spin, voices to be raised – and at times, thankfully, God to be glorified. But they also provide an arena for the speculator, the entrepreneur, the pseudospiritual and the charlatan. The whole area of the miraculous is a minefield when it comes to both personal and public morality and integrity.

However, an idea must not be judged worthy or unworthy merely by seeing who its devotees or practitioners are. Nor should we blindly go along with current philosophy, which asks, 'What's the point?' when we should be asking, 'What's the truth?'

In order to get closer to the truth I will endeavour carefully to demolish the empty derelict shells of past experience and clear away their rubble, for one cannot build afresh on the dubious foundations of the past.

I well remember how everyone thrilled at the idea when architects proposed building a new supermarket in our town. That was, until they realised that a small but beautiful old delicatessen would have to be demolished to make way for the new project. In the end the builders and architects won the day and the old place had to be knocked down. In truth, the small shop had become increasingly ineffective, expensive to maintain and was in fact going out of business. But despite that, many tried sentimentally to hang on like grim death to this property – something that was no longer a going concern.

The individual Christian life and the witness of the contemporary church both face a similar issue. Periodically we need to re-examine our foundations. Sometimes the awkward truth confronts us: Demolition is vital if the Christian perspective – its truth, theology and practice – is going to be rebuilt and stand out in the hedonistic, competitive age in which we live.

Following Jesus' way

'A respectable church will never turn this nation back to God,' a colleague of mine said recently. I'm inclined to agree with him. For too long, in order to gain an ear, we have made it our aim to conform to the world we find ourselves in, rather than transforming it. Or if that has not been our aim it has certainly been the result. The trouble is, although the redis-covery of signs and wonders and healings brings great honour to God and credit to the gospel, as well as to the church, it is often also a messy business, with many mistakes, apparently unanswered prayers and disappointments.

As over the next few years we find our way through this maze, I pray that the gospel will be preached in power, the church will wake up to its responsibilities – to be a blessing to this nation – and that with 'signs following' today's disciples of Christ will live, preach and teach the best news that this world has ever heard.

The gospel is not merely a set of rational propositions coupled with moral idealism (though it has both features), it is also full of the supernatural, mysterious and powerful abilities of God to heal the sick, deliver the demonised, perform the unexplainable, confound clever know-alls of our day, and honour the unsophisticated of this world. That has always been Jesus' way. Therefore it is the kingdom way – for this is Jesus' kingdom, it is his world and it is his time.

Gerald Coates
Esher
Surrey

A PERSONAL PAST

The prayer of faith?

'We pray for our brother laid on a bed of sickness, that thou wilt lay thy healing hand upon him. We pray that he will be swiftly returned to full health and strength – if it be according to thy will.'

It all sounded so spiritual. It was a sort of 'We'd like him to get better – it would be rather nice if you (God) did too' prayer. However, it seemed that knowing God's mind was incredibly difficult. His ways were indeed past finding out – especially when it came to healing! One can still go to evangelical, not to say non-evangelical, prayer meetings where this sort of praying goes on. In fact I not only grew up in this atmosphere, I was well and truly convinced of it and even prayed such prayers myself.

Of course it is true that most of those who pray in this way are absolutely sincere. They really would like to see God moving in power, both for the benefit of the sick and for God's glory. But what happened in our Assembly was that most of our prayer meetings were full of genuine sincerity and compassion but very little power. The 'If it be according to thy will' philosophy always left a back door open for the person who got worse or died (and often they did!). We reasoned that if God heard our prayers and the person got better, we should of course thank God. If such an answer went so far as to defy all the medical predictions, we gave God glory for a 'miracle cure'. (Such things did in fact occasionally take place.) If on the other hand the person didn't get better (which was more often the case), or took three years to get better or even died, we reasoned that God had had a 'better way' or 'greater purpose' than making them well again.

A strange reaction

Years ago a particular theology of suffering and sickness
crept into the church and ate its way into its heart. In its own
way it was itself a sickness. It caused us to suffer from a
curious form of double think. On the one hand we accepted
that our sickness was part of God's will for our lives. To
reinforce the lesson we were told great stories of how the
diseased person was being taught by the Holy Spirit. On the
other hand most of these sick people were strangely resistant
to God's will: they desperately stuffed tablets down their
throats, injected themselves with this, that and the other,
and saw the doctor as regularly as possible.

I couldn't work it out. If it was God's will that people were
sick and that major lessons were being learnt, why were they
so keen on getting better? Why were they like spiritual
truants trying to escape the lessons they should be learning
or treating them like a detention which they had to go to after
school had finished for the day? To ask such questions
amounted to irreverent arrogance, but my confusion was
genuine.

Putting the right pieces together?

One reason for the success of this theology of suffering is that
it fits in very well with another piece of the theological jigsaw
puzzle.

The piece in question is an interpretation of scripture
about scripture.

When you read the New Testament you learn about how
Jesus went around healing the sick. He even told his disciples
to do the same and gave them the authority and training they
would need to do it after he had gone back to his Father in
heaven.

Some people see the signs and wonders and healings that
Jesus performed as the proof that he was God's Son – signs of
his divinity. Nowadays people are more inclined to see these
things as signs of his kingdom – part of the good news of the

gospel. This fits the picture better because the disciples were enabled by the Spirit to perform miracles too. During the growth and establishment of the early church the disciples were able to perform signs and wonders and healings as they took the gospel 'into all the world'.

From some of Paul's letters we learn that he, as an apostle, and various members of the churches he founded – both leaders and others – were gifted with supernatural powers by God's Holy Spirit (the Spirit of Jesus), even if (as at Corinth) they were in need of teaching about the right uses of these gifts.

Later we will see that there are three positions about the miraculous. Here it is sufficient to note that only the people belonging to the position that rules out miracles altogether would not accept the account just given. For those who hold either of the other positions, the problem arises over the question whether the gifts available to the early church are still available to the twentieth-century church.

People with the same strong commitment to and love of the scriptures part company at this point. Some, like myself, cannot see where it is taught that the gifts were only for the disciples of the apostolic church. Others appeal to 1 Corinthians 13, where Paul says that although, faith, hope and love remain, one day all the gifts will cease. For them, when the scriptures were completed (the perfect came) there was no further need for signs and wonders and other spiritual gifts (the imperfect) whose purpose was to validate the gospel. Scripture would provide all the proof that was needed.

There are several reasons why this will not hold water.

1   *It is not clear that Paul is referring to the scriptures at all.* What he is talking about is the time when, after the Lord's return, we will know him 'as we ought'. At that time we will have no need of prophecies, words of knowledge, the gift of tongues and other such phenomena. Until then such sources of revelation, including the Bible itself, will continue.

2   *There seems to be a misunderstanding of the point of the gifts.* As

noted above, the consensus used to be that the miraculous healings and other wonders that Jesus performed were for the express purpose of proving his divinity. That position is now no longer upheld so widely, and with good reason. There are, for example, records of other wonder-workers who were around at the same time as Jesus. No one would claim that *their* miracles proved their divinity – a position, incidentally, that they were loath to claim anyway. Also, Jesus' divinity, although maintained by the New Testament, was not obvious to his followers or his enemies during his ministry. His teaching and actions were to some extent enigmatic and he even appears to have wanted to 'quieten down' those who realised he was the Messiah and God's Son.

In the same way – implying a kind of divine pragmatism – advocates of this position misunderstand the point of the spiritual gifts that God gave to the early church. Their line is that the gifts were historically limited, that they were a kind of stop-gap measure that God used until he had supervised the completion of the New Testament writings and their canonisation.

But the gifts must have more significance than this. The gifts and the fruits of the Holy Spirit are an integral part of Christian experience in the New Testament. When someone becomes a Christian he is adopted into God's family and shares in the Holy Spirit (whether you want to call this 'baptism' or being 'filled' with the Holy Spirit and whether you see this as a once-for-all package received at the time of conversion or a supplementary or 'second blessing' experience that occurs later is not important). This entails being given a new nature and undergoing a reorientation of one's life to God's will, but it also means receiving the power and gifts of the Holy Spirit. In the same way that Jesus' works were an integral part of the inbreaking kingdom of God, the Holy Spirit's gifts are integral to Christian experience – not utilities that are designed to be rendered obsolete by scripture. If that were the case, scripture perhaps ought to be elevated to part of the Godhead – certainly the work of the Spirit would become almost redundant. It doesn't seem right that we should expect to develop the fruits of the Spirit, but no longer expect to receive his gifts.

Surely also, part of the problem is the unhealthy preoccupation with the more spectacular gifts (and I'm referring to both sides of the divide within contemporary evangelicalism): we would be reluctant to say that gifts like administration and counselling were limited to the New Testament era. We need to get our perspectives in order here.

3   *It implies a kind of dispensationalism.* Strictly dispensationalism is a coherent doctrinal system that had its heyday at the end of the last and in the first half of this century. It divided the whole history of salvation into various seemingly watertight compartments, although there was a common theme: covenant. God made various covenants with different biblical figures (Adam, Noah, Moses, David, etc.) and at different times. This approach to biblical truth is a systematic one that threatens to strait-jacket God's revelation and his ways of relating to his people. He seems to deal with people differently at different times; perhaps the most fundamental difference being that between the law and the gospel.

The danger that the advocates of the historically limited position run is similar to that of full-blown dispensationalism. God's methods are linked to specific times and needs: the gifts were necessary, for reasons already hinted at, during the time of Jesus' ministry and the growth of the early church; they are no longer needed.

Again I am forced back to some basic questions relating to God and the way he works: What has changed that makes God's gifts and signs and wonders necessary to the life of the early church but does not require them for its subsequent history? Has God's gospel changed? Has the nature of God's kingdom changed?

Enough is enough!

In my Brethren days, we went out 'on the doors' evangelising, but we didn't expect anybody to be converted – and they weren't! We reasoned that the world was getting worse and that people were becoming hardened to the gospel. Really, what we had was bad news, not good news. If you were sick there was no healing. If you were demonised there was no deliverance. If there was no faith in those we visited for specific needs, we couldn't give a word that would create faith. No wonder our church became smaller and smaller, and we gave up hope. There is nothing sadder than a church that has lost hope.

But there came a time when I became angry at my sin of unbelief, angry with Satan, and angry with sickness. I saw sickness not as part of God's purpose (though he can use anything for his purpose), but as part of the diabolical, twisted nature of Satan to 'steal and kill and destroy' (John 10:10). He steals health and wholeness, killing off faith and vibrant relationships, in order to destroy God's plan to populate the earth with holy men and women.

Not only in Britain, but throughout the world, there is a growing hatred of sin, Satan, sickness and disease. Unless we hate the works of Satan we will never be able to engage ourselves in true spiritual warfare. Spiritual warfare has to do with concrete situations. It is absurd (as happens in certain circles) to pray against the 'Prince of Great Britain' or the 'Prince over Brixton' when there is demonic activity in our own homes, churches and situations left unattended.

A shock to the system

However, this kind of thinking was a million miles away from my own experience at the time. With an inbred indoctrination against Pentecostals, indeed against anything remotely emotional, I became more and more frustrated. But this holy hatred of what Satan had done to people's lives began to break out. Eventually I found myself invited to a small conference by friends who were aware of my growing dissatisfaction with a gospel which had been limited to words and a church which restricted itself to maintenance rather than growth.

At this event recently written songs were sung – which was

quite a shock to my 'hymn and prayer sandwich' mentality –
and conference members fasted during the day (whereas I
had never missed a meal in my life!). But the worst was to
come. At one point somebody spoke in a language I didn't
understand. In my naivety I simply thought we had a
foreigner in the conference! When somebody then prayed in
English (in fact they gave an interpretation of the 'tongue') it
still didn't click. It was not until someone said, 'I've just had
a vision' that I panicked – these were the sort of things I'd
been warned against! Like many others, I'd been brought up
to believe that we should be afraid of everybody who didn't
believe the same as we did – especially Roman Catholics and
Pentecostals! The Roman Catholics, it was inferred, were
demons in disguise (particularly the priests) and Pentecostals took their clothes off in the meetings, swung from the
lights and did cartwheels up the wall! I say 'inferred' because
nobody actually ever said that – but as one great preacher
said, 'You can tell an awful lot from a church not only by
what it says, but by what it doesn't say. And by not only what
it says and doesn't say, but by what it *infers* in what it says
and doesn't say!'

Horrified by this experience, but wanting to understand
such things better, for the next twelve months I read every
book I could on the subjects of the Holy Spirit, healing, signs
and wonders. Frankly, in the late 1960s there was not much
around anyway. But I did read everything I could get my
hands on, from the classic Pentecostal David du Plessis'
books, to those by John Stott, the gifted Anglican Bible
teacher. But reading didn't give me the answers I was
looking for: regarding the baptism in the Spirit, the fullness
of the Spirit and the gifts of the Spirit I became even more
confused.

A new experience

There is nevertheless nothing like a dose of experience to
change one's theology. One day I was riding on my bicycle,
singing one of Wesley's fine hymns. 'Finish then Thy new

salvation,' I happily exclaimed, 'Pure and spotless let us be,
let us see Thy whole salvation – keyayandasadavoostoo!'
Somewhat shocked, I paused, reflected and thought, 'Well,
that's not in the hymnbook!' It was all rather confusing. Was
this the baptism in the Holy Spirit? Was it the release of the
Spirit? Did I make it up? Whatever had happened I rushed
home, leapt upstairs (two at a time) and grabbed a pencil
and pad. How do you write 'keyayandasadavoostoo'? Does it
begin with a 'C' or a 'K'? I still don't know – I'm only
guessing!

For some weeks, perhaps even months, I wondered about
what had happened to me. I didn't know anyone else who
spoke in tongues – or that I could be *sure* spoke in tongues.
The issue was extremely sensitive. Only once before had I
heard someone speak in tongues – and then I thought he was
a foreigner!

In conversation

Eventually I contacted a speaker who I knew had 'Pentecostal' connections. He had once spoken to me at a small
conference. He kindly visited my home that evening.

It was dark and I was nervous. He too was in the dark
about the whole thing – so he was also very nervous! 'I need
to be filled with the Spirit,' I said with some hesitancy. 'I
have read all the right books but I'm totally confused!' He
smiled.

'I don't know whether I have been baptised in the Holy
Spirit or not,' I continued. In desperation I confessed, 'I just
want to be filled up with God.' He gently reminded me that I
knew the scriptures about being filled with the Holy Spirit,
even though in my Assembly I had received teaching against
the gifts of the Spirit, he felt that further teaching on the
subject was not in order. I agreed.

'Are you sure you don't speak in tongues already?' he
asked. I denied my previous experience to make sure I got
the real thing now! 'I feel you do,' he persisted. 'No,' I said,
assuring him that if I did, I would hardly ask him over to

pray for me. But he questioned me further. Eventually I admitted, 'Well – I have had this rather strange experience.' He listened, nodded, smiled again and gave me a knowing look. 'Have you spoken in tongues since then?' he enquired. I told him I had not. 'Do you know your trouble?' he asked. I felt it best to admit that I didn't. He went on to say that my mind had controlled me for years and that when something happened which I couldn't explain I ignored it. He was right. He went on to quote Christ: 'Whoever believes in me, streams of life-giving water will pour out from his heart' (John 7:38 GNB). (Now, several years later, I realise that the mind is a vital part of our make-up, but is not meant to be the source of our Christian lives.)

Then he laid hands on me, prayed for me to be filled with the Holy Spirit and released me from mental domination. Whether 'keyayandasadavoostoo' came into things, I can't remember – but a heavenly language poured out of me. He encouraged me to speak in tongues regularly to 'edify' myself. He also advised me about being discreet as to who I told (this was back in 1969) because not too many would be sympathetic with my testimony.

Far from being a 'second blessing' or the ultimate experience, it became a door that led me out into a whole new world of faith, vision, prayer and love. To this day I don't know whether I was 'baptised in the Spirit' or 'released in the Spirit' (as it is sometimes called). All I know is that I experienced God's love in a wonderful way and wanted to dedicate my energies to his purpose and intentions for my life. Filled and released with the Holy Spirit I certainly was and, nearly twenty years later, I am happy to live with that. I pray in tongues almost every day and have seen thousands experience the same since then – from doctors, lawyers and computer programmers to artists, housewives, entertainers and children.

It was this experience, coupled with my understanding of scripture, that led me into my growing interest in the kingdom rather than the church. Soon, my somewhat level-headed wife began to ask God for more of the Holy Spirit. We

shared with a few close friends what had happened to us.
They began to read the scriptures, pray for a fresh experience
of the Holy Spirit and without exception were not disappointed. Most of those people are now in leadership roles
in the church, and have been for years.

The healing sign

A short while later, but still long before the plethora of books
and cassettes on the work and gifts of the Spirit became
popular, something else happened. It was to be the first
healing sign I experienced.

My hands were covered with warts. Doctors had told me
that the treatment was simple: they could be 'pulled out or
burned out'. I decided to postpone such pain. Eventually,
though, they became an ugly embarrassment. One day,
when I was out riding my bicycle – yet again, I prayed,
'Lord, I would very much appreciate it if you would heal me
of these warts.' It was not the most faith-filled prayer I've
ever heard, but it was real. God didn't answer my prayer
immediately, despite my feeling they would all drop out on
the spot! But, having been plagued by these warts for several
years, I was about to experience another evidence of God's
love and power. Sorting mail in the Post Office one day, I
fingered a wart (a bad habit acquired over the years), but it
had disappeared! I looked down, and not one was left – every
one had gone. Fifteen years later I have not had one return.
This was an early evidence of what was to be the norm, a
small sign that I wondered about and now thank God for.

In conclusion – a new beginning

This potted history is relevant, not just for me but also for
others. These struggles and experiences were part of a
national and international struggle out of 'church' into
'kingdom'. Many have emerged out of apathy into genuine
concern, paralysis into action, a low level of faith into specific
faith and from pessimism into optimism. It was and still is a

journey out of predictable behaviour into a dynamic of faith, prayer and morality akin to what one reads of in the Acts of the Apostles.

I am not, therefore, waving a flag for something that I have always believed in. Quite the opposite. Entering the kingdom is always through struggle, tribulation, disappointment and hard work. Failures, unanswered questions and total mysteries abound. But sufficient has been experienced and enough known of scripture to motivate a growing array of 'nobodies' to declare that 'He gives us signs.'

As has been said before, there is nothing like a dose of experience to change one's theology. Not only to change it, but to fine-tune it and close the credibility gap between what we say we believe about our God and how we meet people's needs. The Spirit is often at work in us long before our theology catches up with what is happening.

This same Spirit of power comes with healing, deliverance, and the miraculous, but he also comes as the Spirit of truth. In fact he can be counted on to lead us into all truth. Only those who aspire after both – sound theology and genuine dynamic experience – will have the right to address themselves to our nation. We cannot lead others if we do not know where we are going. So it is vital that God's Holy Spirit leads us.

SCHOOLS OF THOUGHT

When it comes to 'signs and wonders' there are three main schools of thought:

1   The miracles recorded in scripture didn't happen then, so they certainly don't happen today either.

2   The Old and New Testament miracles did happen, but because we now have the scriptures, miracles are unnecessary so they don't happen today.

3   The miracles recorded in both the Old and New Testaments did happen, and because God's nature hasn't changed miracles must therefore happen today.

1 The sceptics

It is hard to see how this first school could represent a *Christian* option at all. If God didn't do amazing and wonderful things, then we'd have to question his nature, rewrite (or heavily edit) scripture and close down the evangelical church.

We would have a God of our own making, powerless, uninvolved and unconcerned with the struggles of humanity. Think of the implications. It would mean that those we currently look on as his most faithful biblical followers were either remarkably deceived or that those who wrote about them in scripture were liars of the worst kind. Jesus would have to be looked on as nothing more than a moral teacher whose kingdom was really just another ethical system. The Holy Spirit would be a benign but ultimately impotent 'influence'. And with no powerful, personal, righteous and loving God, and no heaven or hell other than of our own making, there would be little purpose in there being a church.

What confusion! With no personal God and no trustworthy word from heaven, with no accurate account of how he acts and what he expects of us, we would be cast adrift in a cold, unfriendly, inexplicable world.

Sadly there are people who hold such views – or ones very like them. Some of them have even been elevated into television personalities and religious pundits. Their message is depressing: 'We can be sure of nothing.' Faith is at sea, or else it *is* the sea and the tide has gone out. Everything gets reduced to morality. But such a view is impoverished. Their God of morality is not the God of scripture who acts on behalf of his faithful and prayerful people. Perhaps we ought not to be surprised that it is this wing of the church that is diminishing most rapidly in numbers throughout Britain. Perhaps we should not be too sorry either.

2 The historically limited

This school typifies where the evangelical church has been for many years. The accuracy and integrity of scripture are upheld and, in the main, it is admitted that God 'could' heal the sick 'if he wished'. Those in this school are not beyond praying for the sick, but would be highly surprised to receive an immediate answer to their prayers.

God performed miracles, they reason, to authenticate Jesus' mission. This, it is argued, applies also to the early church. But now we have the Bible to guide us. Therefore we do not expect to see the Holy Spirit doing such things with regularity today. But scripture itself gives no hint that when the canon of scripture was completed, the demonised would have to remain so, and the sick simply 'learn lessons' or merely find grace to remain sick or die. It needs to be said that scripture is given alongside the miraculous, not instead of it!

God is not unaffected by the cries of his people or indeed of humanity as a whole. But James made it clear that often we don't get because we don't ask: 'You do not have what you want because you do not ask God for it' (James 4:2). We will not ask if we don't expect God to answer.

The result of this school of thought is now clear. Instead of warring warriors we have weary worshippers in the church. Instead of a people who believe *in* God we believe in things *about* God. Instead of a redeemed community taking ground from Satan in all manner of lives and situations, we still expect things to get worse and the church to get smaller.

The sad truth is that in Britain we *are* getting smaller! One factor must be our predominantly white, largely middle-class western European view of the church – and of Christianity in general – that is wedded to the outlook of school number two.

By contrast, look at the church in China. The growth rate there (and in Africa, South America and elsewhere for that matter) is astonishing. It too is related to a particular vision of the church and Christianity. But not the one we are content with. In 1947 only one million people in China were thought to be 'born again' believers. By the close of the 1970s, out of a thousand million Chinese, some thirty to fifty million are regarded as born again believers.

True, the Chinese church has suffered incredibly for many decades. Families have been divided. Leaders have been imprisoned. Christian literature has been relentlessly confiscated. Buildings have been closed and demolished and resources have been stripped from the Christian community. However, in this terribly hurtful situation their cry has gone up to God. The injustice of the situation, and the mass of human tragedy, has caused them to look beyond themselves and their immediate resources. And so, with signs and wonders, God has answered those prayers.

Perhaps from our western perspective the Chinese church lacks order, theological understanding and a constitution upon which it can base its affairs. But their suffering has produced a humility, a dependence on God and a simplicity of faith that is rare in the sophisticated west. Friends of mine who have recently returned from China tell me that they have never wept so much as when they witnessed the beauty and power of God on the one hand and the suffering and deprivation of the church on the other.

Those in the second school believe in the miraculous power of God in the same way that their children believe in the tooth fairy or Santa Claus – there are historical reasons why the beliefs arose, but they are inappropriate in a different day and age. How different this is to the attitude of Chinese and Korean believers who, because they could do no other, have trusted God at his word and have adopted a bold approach to the preaching of the gospel and demonstrated an expectancy that God will answer prayer if the church finds faith.

A major point at which the second school's true colours come out is over the issue of sickness and health. The view is one we've already noted and, as I said earlier, it is the one I grew up with.

This theology of sickness is one of resignation. When we are sick it is reckoned to be God's will as he teaches us so much through such situations. The blessed school of learning becomes the blessed school of sickness. In fact – and this is almost perverse – to become sick might logically be viewed as being more spiritual than being healthy. It is surely seen in some circles as providing God greater scope for teaching us spiritual lessons. There is no doubt that God is able to communicate his love, truth and 'lessons' when we are attentive because we are suffering ill health. Sickness limits travel, socialising and other commitments. It also weakens our natural senses and defences, so it is often true that those who have suffered the most are more sensitive to the Holy Spirit and his ministry and are therefore more spiritually attuned.

But such experiences must never in and of themselves be made the foundation of our theology of God. And we must not end up in the absurd position, which I mentioned in the last chapter and which is surely hypocritical, or at least a case of trying to have your cake and eating it, of claiming on the one hand that our sickness is of God and for our spiritual benefit while on the other hand dashing from doctor to specialist and stuffing ourselves with all types of medication at all points between. If it really is God's will that we are sick, why try and wriggle out of it?

Those who hold to the views of the second school must go back to scripture for a proper understanding of health and wholeness.

Don't misunderstand my attitude to medicine and the medical profession. I'm not 'against' modern medicine, but I am against two tendencies that people have towards it. The first makes the mistake of seeing doctors as healers. The second restricts *all* healing to them. The Bible provides a balance between these two attitudes. It sees a place for medicine and medical advice, but it limits it.

It is interesting to note, for example, that Jesus had a physician on his team – Dr Luke – and that the apostle Paul told his student Timothy to take 'a little wine' for his stomach's sake. Eating properly, and following medical advice and medication are not to be seen as the fruit of unbelief and sin or as God's second best. Indeed the medical profession has done the Christian cause a tremendous amount of good both at home and abroad. It is not a matter of either/or.

The apostle Paul, in 1 Corinthians 12 tells us of the gifts of 'healing'. We must not reduce them to the medical profession – such a philosophy leaves a lot to be desired. Christian doctors in particular are doing a great deal to alleviate suffering and through their work bring Christ to people. That cannot be in question. But we must be careful that we do not call agnostic and atheistic General Practitioners healers, never mind healers in the name of Christ.

Let's thank God for the medical profession, for their wisdom, care and skills. We must pray for Christian doctors, that through their caring profession the love of God and perhaps the words of Christ will reach into people's lives. If we listened to our doctors, disciplined ourselves and cared for one another a little more, perhaps as Christians we wouldn't waste so much of their time. But the medical profession is not a panacea for all ills. There is no miracle cure for every disease and whether it be the flu, cancer or AIDS, medical advice must go hand in hand with prayer and faith in God's ability to do what the medical profession has no power to do.

3 A better way

It is clear, I hope, from the nature of my comments on the second school that I have now found a better way – one which does not relegate signs and wonders and healings to a bygone age but which sees the same God giving the same gifts for the same purpose by the same Spirit as he did in first-century Palestine.

Scripture seems clear on the issue of sickness: it is God's will for his holy people to minister healing. It is God's will for sinners, and especially for unbelievers, to be healed. It is worth noting here that Jesus never prayed for his disciples to be healed. James, one of Jesus' friends, says however, 'Is there anyone who is ill? He should send for the church elders, who will pray for him and rub olive-oil on him in the name of the Lord. This prayer made in faith will heal the sick person; the Lord will restore him to health, and the sins he has committed will be forgiven' (James 5: 14–15 GNB).

Satan, on the other hand, came to 'steal and kill and destroy' (John 10:10). But God's way is the opposite. Salvation makes whole. God's way is health, wholeness and harmony; Satan's way is to break down, wreck, rob and infect.

Read what the Bible says was Jesus' approach:

Jesus went all over Galilee, teaching in the synagogues, preaching the Good News about the Kingdom, and healing people who had all kinds of disease and sickness. The news about him spread through the whole country of Syria, so that people brought to him all those who were sick, suffering from all kinds of diseases and disorders:

people with demons, and epileptics, and paralytics – and Jesus healed them all. Large crowds followed him from Galilee and the Ten Towns, from Jerusalem, Judaea, and the land on the other side of the Jordan (Matthew 4:23–25).

Notice how Jesus' ministry was one that challenged and broke the effects of the fall. As individuals and as a society, we have fallen from God's original intention for our lives. That has consequences. If we abandon God and his moral order then disorder breaks out at every level – physically, mentally, emotionally, relationally, economically and governmentally. We see this today on every hand in every nation. But through healing and deliverance Jesus expressed and communicated the nature of his Father in heaven. Such events were part of the reason, if not the major reason, why crowds followed him and listened to him with rapt attention.

But there is no quick way to faith. Even the disciples had failures. On one occasion Jesus made it clear that certain demons only come out through prayer and fasting. So the effects of the fall, of sin and man's rebellion against God are all around us. We are in a battle, and due to our own limitations and understanding there are battles we lose. The writer to the Hebrew Christians tells us of heroes of faith who escaped death and glorified God. But he also speaks of those who were sawn in half and glorified God in their death, as did the thousands who died in the arenas, mauled by lions and mutilated by gladiators.

For Peter in prison there was deliverance. For Paul it would seem, as he came near to life's end, that this was not the case. We are on dangerous ground if we say that Peter had more faith than Paul. Jesus, the perfect man who was also perfect God, did not only perform miracles, heal the sick and deliver the demonised, he offered himself up on several occasions to the verbal and physical abuse of those who were subject to the fallenness and depravity of human nature.

Jesus didn't leave it there. He *transferred* his power to his disciples and commissioned them to do the same. 'Believers will be given the power to perform miracles: they will drive out demons in my name; they will speak in strange tongues . . .' (Mark 16:17 GNB). Their ministry and the record in the Acts of the Apostles (which despite appearances actually covers between thirty and sixty years) demonstrates this point. God's healing powers have always been at work – even in dark days. Nowhere are we taught that the Bible, when completed, would spell the end of the church's ministry to release the demonised or heal the sick.

We must thank God for scripture and not minimise its importance. But we must not pretend that the fact that we now have scripture places an embargo on the miraculous, as if God, having shown by the biblical record that he is a God who acts to deliver his people and work wonders to the praise of his glory, now says that we've seen enough of his character, or that he is no longer capable of performing miracles, or that he has changed his kingdom's priorities.

We must be honourable at this point. We must not let fear, unanswered questions and the possibility of failure lead us to disregard part of our mission and our resources. We must fight our fear and our reservations with the biblical facts.

Remember the people for whom our message is to be good news. To the sick the good news is not Habakkuk, it is healing. To the demonised the good news is not Deuteronomy, it is deliverance. God is looking for an active army not a confused congregation. He is raising up a participating community of faith-filled people – ordinary people – to do his will. It is not good enough to mask our fear by saying, 'Conservative theology is at hand' or 'Traditional Christianity is at hand!' Our local, national and international cry must be, 'The kingdom of God is at hand.'

Where God's rule is evident there is power – power to heal, reconcile and to save. Jesus was given the Spirit 'without measure' (John 3:34 NASB). We, however, *are* given 'a measure' and must recognise our limitations. This should make us dependent on God, and also on those he puts around us. They will have a different 'measure' to make up our deficiencies.

God clearly did signs and wonders throughout both Old and New Testament times. We do not have the slightest indication that he would cease this wonderful, redemptive ministry when the canon of scripture was completed. To say that God 'could' do mighty things but that he usually doesn't begs the question, 'Why?'

That is a question to which this school of interpretation does not seem able to provide a satisfactory answer. Like the attitude to healing, what often occurs is a tendency to doublethink. For example, I heard of a London chapel at which an exorcism was practised recently. What was strange was the minister's attitude. 'God doesn't have anything to do with this sort of thing,' he said. In fact he did not believe in miracles at all. Yet, nevertheless, he went ahead and performed the exorcism service! Perhaps his attitude to the demonic was not typical of all those who belong to the second school, but his inconsistency was.

Many have firsthand experience of the first two schools. The first leaves us with a God of our own making. One who lives in our heads only to disappear when we die – a God who lives only in our fantasies. The second leaves us with a God who truly did amazing things and performed wonderful acts of mercy through his incarnate Son and his biblical followers, but does so no longer. But there is an alternative that is still available: the third school. Although it still has its problems, triumphalistic followers and a measure of unanswered questions, I take my arrival at this position to be a form of graduation. My faith in God's ability grows, and I now stand convinced that both God and scripture point us to a future of hope, not to a diminishing gospel message that is reduced to words and oratory.

Different sorts of miracles

It would be good at this stage to ask an important question: If the God who did the miracles recorded in scripture still does them, what then is a miracle?

Not every unexpected occurrence is a miracle; so despite

what my friends may say, it would not be right to say that if I
remembered people's names it was a miracle! So what is a
miracle, then? Biblically speaking, a miracle is not just a big
set-piece for show or entertainment. It does not merely have
a utility value either (for example, to provide a means of
escape from a tight spot). A miracle is a sign that captures the
attention and points to something or someone else. It causes
wonder, both in the sense of awe and because it causes one to
stop and think about what it is meant to signify.

There are different classes of miracles, depending how we
understand their nature.

First of all there are miracles of timing. Naturally occur-
ring events happen at particularly opportune times. The
calming of the storm when the disciples boat was in danger of
sinking and the finding of the coin in the fish's mouth to pay
the temple tax are miracles of timing. Many healings that
occur today may fall into this category. The point is that the
timing is miraculous, but the event may be one that would
ordinarily happen at a different speed.

The second type of miracle consists of those things that can
already be, or at least one day will be capable of being,
scientifically explained. The fact that one can explain such
events does not make them less miraculous.

For example, according to Joshua 10, during a battle
Joshua told the sun to stand still and it did. From our
viewpoint more explanations are available than Joshua had.
For instance, we now know that the sun does not revolve
around the earth, so we might want to say that it was
actually the earth that stopped moving rather than the
sun. But although we may be able to explain the mech-
anics of the physical elements involved in the miracle, the
central point remains – the day of the battle was miraculously prolonged by God's direct intervention on behalf of
his people.

Science may underscore the relative ignorance (viewed
from our privileged position) of the biblical characters, but it
does not remove the miracle. When we give our account
based on our somewhat limited and ignorant perspectives

God does not always crash into our humanity with his view of things.

The third category of miracle has to do with things that are entirely beyond our current scientific understanding and may continue to be. These include feeding five thousand people from virtually nothing, turning water into very good wine, walking on water and, of course, raising to life those who died several days previously.

Luke, a trained physician and articulate historian, records many of those instances. Among other things, these records show that our creator is not bound by his creation. For although God created and sustains his work, he is not bound by time, for he exists outside of time. God is a timeless God who works in time because he has chosen to. Hence on occasion, God says, 'Before they call, I will answer' (Isaiah 65:24 AV).

It has been said that scientific laws are really the laws of man anyway. That doesn't mean that they are like statute book laws which society has decided are beneficial for the general wellbeing. Instead it means that on the basis of scientific observations and experiments we notice that certain things happen repeatedly according to a predictable pattern. Scientists formulate 'laws' on the basis of these things. They serve as explanations of what happens and what will happen. But they are subject to revision. A theory cannot explain everything. Sometimes sufficient examples occur to make it necessary to revise or even throw out the theory and its laws and replace them with another model.

The nature of scientific laws means that some miracles may fall right outside their range and must therefore be inexplicable, unlike the first and second kinds of miracles.

What are signs and wonders for?

Even if some miracles do break such laws and remain unexplained, they are not an end in themselves. Instead they are a vital means of communicating God's love, care and concern for us all.

While such miraculous events can become a substitute for a living relationship with God, we in Europe and most 'civilised' parts of the world are not in danger of such idolatry. Faith for miracles is low, and in many churches frowned upon. Prayers for a miracle and actually believing for one are two different things. A friend of mine told me he was praying for his neighbours, hoping they would find faith, find Christ and become Christians. 'Can you see it happening?' I enquired. 'Never in a million years!' he replied. His prayers were well intentioned. Unfortunately, they were without hope or faith. In fact, even if his neighbours had become Christians it is unlikely he would have been ready to nurture them in their faith. He wasn't expecting his prayers to be answered.

Answered prayers, miraculous interventions and 'signs and wonders' are given primarily because God loves to interact and have a relationship with those who have faith. God does not intervene in every hurt, injustice and disaster. If he did we would cease to be anything other than puppets – the victims of God's benevolence whether we wanted to be or not. He is wanting to answer our prayers and develop a relationship. God also gives us 'signs and wonders' to feed our faith, humble our hearts and to keep them tender towards himself and those around us.

To be truly balanced and healthy we must be faithful to what God has said, but grow in faith for God to work in powerful ways in the future:

. . . we ought to pay much closer attention than ever to the truths that we have heard, lest in any way we drift past [them] and slip away. For if the message given through angels [that is, the Law spoken by them to Moses] was authentic and proved sure, and every violation and disobedience received an appropriate [just and adequate] penalty, how shall we escape [appropriate retribution] if we neglect and refuse to pay attention to such a great salvation [as is now offered to us, letting it drift past us forever]? For it was declared at first by the Lord [Himself],

and it was confirmed to us and proved to be real and
genuine by those who personally heard [Him speak].
[Besides these evidences] it was also established and
plainly endorsed by God, Who showed His approval of
it by signs and wonders and various miraculous manifes-
tations of [His] power and by imparting the gifts of the
Holy Spirit [to the believers] according to His own will
(Hebrews 2:1–4 Amplified Version).

Wonderful ignorance!

At one time, I – like many others – asked: 'Where has God
got to?' Well, he was waiting, in humility and power, for us to
find faith for him to do what he has done throughout history.

True, God often works despite our faith, not because of it.
But a faith-filled life, family, church and nation will see more
signs and wonders than those who have relegated such a God
to the Middle East of two thousand years ago. The church
that is on the march, growing in power and in love, is the
church that has taken God at his word. God's people in
Africa, China, South America, India, and in so many other
places are growing numerically because they have done just
this. Some are totally ignorant of schools one and two! In
ignorance and faith, not knowing any better (or worse) they
have seen God's love, care and word honoured through signs
and wonders.

In Britain the situation is different. A church like ours with
few signs and wonders, is unlikely to survive this century in
Britain. A church that doesn't believe its God will deliver the
demonised, heal the sick and answer prayer has little good
news. A church that believes in an impersonal, uncaring God
who may have done mighty things in the past and who may
even do mighty things in the world to come, is hopeless. Only
a church that can love Christ, pursue truth and believe for
God's power to break into the present order of things has a
vital message for Britain. That message is clear: for the guilty
it is forgiveness; for the sick it is healing; for the oppressed
and the demonised it is deliverance; for the poor it is the

redistribution of resources and wealth (Luke 4:18–19; Ephesians 4:28). But that message will be possible only if we invite the rule of God – his kingdom – into our lives.

THE KINGDOM OF GOD

There were two things that seemed to motivate and direct the ministry of Christ. One was his Father in heaven, the other was the kingdom of God on the earth. He barely mentioned the church, but his Father and the kingdom were on his lips constantly. He longed to reach those who felt they were beyond God's love and mercy. He healed the sick, delivered the demonised and gave hope to the hopeless for this very reason. As has been mentioned it is not recorded that Jesus ever prayed for healing or deliverance for his committed disciples. But he was intent on revealing what his Father was like to those in ignorance. He intended them to see God's miracles as examples of his nature and rule.

Two of the major hurdles to spreading our Christian influences need attention. One is to do with how we convey the nature of 'Father'. The other has to do with how he rules, intervenes and participates in the suffering of humanity. The church should clearly convey both the Fatherly, merciful nature of God and the moral nature of his rule. Today, the church has to decide whether it will sink in what it's got or swim with change. Allowing the kindness of God and his powerful government – his kingdom – to motivate and direct our church and ministries will create the greatest and best changes. It is insufficient to live proper little Christian lives which fail to convey God's wonderful nature and purpose in society.

The attitude which seems to obey the unwritten commandment, 'Thou shalt present a good image for God, and kid thyself – as thou kiddest thy neighbour' has nothing to do with the life of the kingdom! God's forgiving nature and his kingdom are evident from the most casual observation of scripture. But God is looking for this generation to fulfil scripture as Jesus in his generation fulfilled scripture. We must embrace God's truth, fatherly heart and power. Without the Bible, how would we see such a clear insight into the nature of God's kingdom? Without those God-breathed unique pieces of literature, how could we know how God intends to reach into 'the outermost parts of the world'? But God wants us to read, learn, absorb and teach scripture by the power of the Spirit. That power is available to take us into realms that, alongside scripture, will help people know what God is like.

> The Bible is God's testimony to his Son. Its purpose is to direct men on divine authority to Jesus as the source of life. The Bible is a signpost. It cannot give life itself. It can only point you to the One in whom light can be found. It's a prescription. It cannot cure sin, but it can specify the medicine that will. It is vital that those of us who call ourselves evangelicals understand this. The Bible is never an end in itself. And if we are ever found treating it as such, we fall into the trap of which some validly accuse us; bibliolatry, worshipping a divine book rather than its divine author.
>
> Of course we value the Bible highly, but we do so because it is the Father's testimony to Jesus ... Bible study can never be an end in itself. It is a pilgrimage intended to lead us to an ever deeper and more intimate knowledge of Christ (Roy Clements, *Introducing Jesus* (Kingsway 1986), p. 57). Thank God for scripture, mercy and power!

Ruling – without us!

The Holy Spirit pays Jesus the highest accolade and brings him glory. Jesus pays the Father the highest accolade and brings him glory. The Bible gives us unique God-given insights into the nature and workings of the Godhead. The

centre of this kingdom is the Father's heart, his word and his
ways. His rule, however, is not wholly dependent on the
church. His 'signs and wonders' do not need to work through
a redeemed life. In truth, he is above all that. So loving
Christian relationships are not the kingdom of God, they are
its *evidence*! Breakfast flying in daily for two million wander-
ing Jews has nothing to do with godliness – rather God
himself. Seas dividing for salvation and closing to drown
Israel's military enemies likewise have little to do with a
heart submitted to God's rule. God rules over and outside of
human action and reaction as well as through them. Jesus'
ministry was successful because, in his own words, 'the Son
. . . does only what he sees his Father doing' (John 5:19 GNB).
Our responsibility is, as one church leader put it, to 'find out
what God is doing in [our] generation and get in on it!' God is
at work in Britain. Let's find out where and serve him there.

Isaiah's prophecy, referring to Jesus the Messiah, 'Of the
increase of his government and peace there will be no end'
(Isaiah 9:7), will in fact come about when this rule is evidenced in people's lives. For Luke records that Jesus' end was
hastened by the cry, 'We do not want this man to reign over us'
(Luke 19:14 NASB). But the end of this present world order will
be hastened when we declare, 'We *will* have this man ruling
over us!' This will be when God's rule is evidenced in power
in the life of the church. He looks today for men and women
who are daily turning from the values of the world to the
values of the kingdom – for those who have stepped out of
darkness and confusion into the light of Christ and the order
of his rule. 'My kingdom is not of this world' (John 18:36), he
said – focusing our attention on the source of his rule. His life
and words demonstrated the redemptive, benevolent optimism of God's kingdom! Peoples fearful or cynical of human
governments need to see the benevolent rule of God.

A kingdom person?

To be a kingdom person means having a kingdom theology.
Acknowledging the true king of space and time will bring

us into direct conflict with all pretenders to his throne. All too often we have been satisfied with a non-threatening, non-kingdom theology. But that sort of theology is a denial of Jesus' rule and right to rule in all the affairs of humanity.

Pretenders are not only those who in their own being reject Christ's rule, they are also the ones who seek to usurp that rule in others. Primarily they are demons who influence and at times control individuals. This is especially true of those who have opened themselves up to the world of the occult and spiritism.

I once prayed for the son of a top naval man. For a time he lived with an American family. As owners of a local restaurant, they ate rather well. But an irrational fear gripped this man: he feared that he may never eat again! One day he purchased six enormous bowls. He used to keep one for cereal at breakfast time, but hid the others. This, he told me, was 'in case the others were smashed or damaged'. He ate like a horse, was as slim as Twiggy, and continually lived with this fear of hunger. I realised that this was not merely psychological, it was a confrontation between God's kingdom of light and Satan's kingdom of darkness. (Some situations are just that.) So we agreed to pray against this bondage to eating. I rebuked the spirit of gluttony, although the young man in question baulked at this. He didn't much believe in demons or anything of that sort. His public school and Anglican background left little room for such apparent absurdities. After prayer in Jesus' name and deliverance from this demonic bondage, he went straight home and smashed his ridiculously large cereal bowls. (They were more like washing-up bowls!) That was over ten years ago; he is now in leadership in one of the churches my team cares for.

This deliverance was an evidence of God's rule. To that young man, the kingdom of God had come. The pretenders were ousted and today that man eats properly and is happily married with children.

Of course some may say that Christians cannot have

demons, to which our reply must be, 'Can demons have Christians?'

Enemies of God's kingdom

It has been said that the nearer one is to Christ, the greater enemy activity will be experienced. The fact that the unconverted are often open to all kinds of influences doesn't mean that believers are automatically immune from them. Just as all people in all places are affected by the Holy Spirit, so all believers are to some degree affected by demons. This is why even believers can so easily become deceived.

Our enemy presently rules virtually uncontrolled in many parts of the world – including many parts of Britain. Worldwide there are over sixteen thousand ethnic groups (around two and a half billion people) that have no church. Only the good news of the rule of God – a rule that delivers people from sin and demonic influence or bondage – will break into the present system of things. A gospel of healing, hope and a wonderful miracle-working God is good news to such people.

Although the precise phrase 'Kingdom of God' does not occur there, its source is found in the Old Testament. The reigning God is prominent in various psalms, for example. The apocalyptic writers, such as Daniel, emphasised God as one who would break into the present world order and establish a new one. Certainly in the New Testament the presence of Jesus meant the presence of the kingdom. After his baptism by John, the anointing by the Holy Spirit and the temptations in the wilderness, Jesus said, 'The right time has come, and the Kingdom of God is near! Turn away from your sins and believe the Good News!' (Mark 1:15 GNB).

The sense of God breaking into the time/space world is seen when Jesus says, 'I tell you, there are some here who will not die until they have seen the Kingdom of God come with power' (Mark 9:1).

The values of the kingdom are also seen when Jesus gives us a glimpse into the age to come.

Then the King will say to the people on the right, 'Come you that are blessed by my Father! Come and possess the kingdom which has been prepared for you ever since the creation of the world. I was hungry and you fed me, thirsty and you gave me a drink; I was a stranger and you received me in your homes, naked and you clothed me; I was sick and you took care of me, in prison and you visited me.'

To explain how this is done he continued, 'I tell you, whenever you did this for one of the least important of these brothers of mine, you did it for me!' (Matthew 25:34–36, 40 GNB).

So the kingdom of God must not be confined to the joys of health and wholeness, miracles and deliverance. Certainly we must pray for more evidence of God's power in those areas, particularly in Britain, but we must not fall into the 'either/or' trap: *either* doing good *or* performing miracles. Many who are doing good have no faith in miracles. But similarly there are many who are asking God to meet needs by miraculous means when we are able to and should be meeting them ourselves. God gives Christians a terrific amount of responsibility and room to develop their ministry to those who are in need. The Christian life consists of love that costs as well as faith that works. Our call to serve God involves personal inconvenience as well as corporate blessing.

The extraordinary power of God must be seen in the context of serving God in the ordinary things of life. Human kindness, acts of self-denial and blessing others with what God has given us are all part of this kingdom. The kingdom has both aspects: it is natural and supernatural; it is full of faith and full of human energies. We must look to God and ask him to do what only he can do as we get on and do what only we can do.

WHERE ARE WE NOW?

Wherever there are people who share the kingdom's values, there will be a mutual attraction. A entirely new type of leadership is emerging. Such leaders have a 'high view' of scripture and preach a gospel of God's overwhelming mercy and grace, which when received causes true repentance. Among such people, with expectations fresh, new and uncluttered, it is not difficult to have faith for healing and wholeness. Just as the reason for the amazing church growth in China, Africa, South America and elsewhere is somehow related to 'signs and wonders', many of us believe it will be so in Britain. This is not merely a matter of what is more exciting; it is rather to do with what we perceive to be God's intention by his Spirit. Those who reduce the kingdom to words are no less God's children and God is clearly blessing them. But these 'signs and wonders' which result in changed lives will open more and more people up to Christ and his rule.

In the 1970s we lost a million church members. We closed a thousand churches and lost two and a half thousand ministers. In the first five years of the 1980s we lost another half million members and we are on target to lose a total of one million by 1990. Some have argued that we are losing 'dead wood'. I am not so convinced. New churches are being opened up, but they are not keeping pace. We have to face it, there is a low level of faith in Britain which is, I believe, directly related to the low level of faith in the church.

While writing this chapter I took part in a BBC Radio 4 programme. It consisted of the presenter, a witch, an Anglican philosopher and myself. Despite clearly stating the evil and danger as well as the utter nonsense of witchcraft, I had a certain sympathy for the witch. She believed in the supernatural and told me that if the church had offered her more than it did, she probably wouldn't be doing what she was. The philosopher, who is on the General Synod, told us that he didn't even believe in demons! But God gets his will done when we plant the kingdom seed. This he kindly enabled me to do, and it was the witch and her husband who wanted to see me for a talk after the programme. 'We have never met a Christian like you,' they said as we waited for our BBC cars to whisk us home. They reckoned that there were about a hundred thousand witches in Britain – yet they also told me that there is a considerable level of dissatisfaction with it, for many of them. It is our role, as God's people – his church – to introduce God and his power to the British scene. They are needed everywhere: in government, the arts, education, business, families, in debates about racism and sexism and even among witches.

Copying the world?

Although the whole world needs the message of the kingdom and the power of God, we must not let the world set the agenda for us. Meeting needs is the fruit of God's kingdom – not its cause. What we must do instead is to increase our own and each other's level of faith in God. Faith-filled people will make for a faith-filled church. In turn a faith-filled church, may bring about a faith-filled society. That is why we must be clear about the nature of sickness.

That must seem like an odd thing to say. What has sickness got to do with it? Well, as I outlined in the first two chapters, the church has got itself into a cleft stick over the issue of health and sickness and how they relate to the will of God. Faith becomes a crucial element in the equation, because on the one hand God's will is that through our time of illness he is able to teach us valuable lessons about himself but on the other hand those who say they believe this run around trying to find ways of minimising the time they are exposed to this influence. Yet God does not want people to be ill. His will is that his people should be healthy. One aspect of the kingdom of God is the gift of healing. It is an integral part of God's message.

Occasionally God's enemies found their health suffered when they opposed him: Pharaoh lost his heir to the throne (Exodus 11:5; 12:29) and Saul was blinded (Acts 9:8), as was Elymas (Acts 13:11). It is also true that, as we grow older, parts wear out! But in both situations God can break into that cycle of things with healing.

God's overwhelming heart for us to be whole is evidenced by the vast majority of cases when he and his disciples brought healing to people. Not all sickness is judgment, as we have already mentioned (for example Timothy and his stomach problems). But health, not sickness, is what we as God's people should be aiming for.

God's general will for the church is that we are well. Yet his permissive will allows sickness because of other factors. Just as his general will is that we do not sin, he nevertheless permits us to sin for other reasons.

The story of Job illustrates the distinction between God's general will and his permissive will. Job was a good man. He enjoyed the blessings of Yahweh. His family seemed close-knit and pleasing to God. His business was an obvious success. He was, in fact, a wealthy man. So what happened?

What happened to Job shows us both the effects of the fall and the nature of battle we are all engaged in – if only we will realise the nature of our warfare as Christians.

Satan, the instigator of the fall, presents himself to God. He had been surveying God's creation in the earth. God draws Satan's attention to Job, to his life and his faith. Here came the challenge. In effect Satan said, 'With all the blessing and favour you have bestowed upon him and his family, who wouldn't serve you?' God knew that Job loved him for who he was, not simply for what he could get out of him. So he permitted Satan to disrupt, destroy and spread disease, but he forbade him from taking Job's life. Satan wanted God to do all of those things and indeed he implicitly challenged him to do so, but God doesn't do that sort of thing. So, within God-given limits, Satan did his worst. The question was to be answered in this man. Would Job serve God simply for who the Lord is or prove that he only pleased God because of what he got out of him?

Early on in the cycle of speeches, Job laments the day of his birth (Job 10:18). He had, after all, lost his business, his staff and most of his family. But he declared that although God *could* deliver him from all of this mess, even if he didn't, he would still trust him. He put his faith in God. However, that doesn't always help us see things from God's perspective. Most of us fail to see things as God sees them even when seeking to honour God. That is why there are so many mysteries in life. We do not see that *we* are the battleground. As someone has said, the battleground doesn't choose where the battle is going to be fought, the commanders of the armies do. Just as Job (one man) became the battleground for the question to be answered, so today the church (God's many-membered corporate man) is the battleground. Do we love and serve God simply for who he is or for what we get out of him? If Satan offered us the same success and wealth would we follow him? This question is being answered daily across the face of the earth.

The Psalmist and the New Testament writers tell us that if we live as God wants us to we should expect health, and a long life. A lot of illnesses are brought on through unnecessary worry and self-imposed pressure, overwork, bitter relationships, tension and sexual promiscuity. When we 'cast our cares on the Lord' or 'walk in the light', when we confess our 'faults to one another' and 'pray for one another', this makes for blessing and health.

We should look forward to health. It is God's will for us. Scripture is also quite clear what we should do as Christians when we are sick: call for our leaders and be ready to confess anything that may be a contributing factor (James 5:14–16).

Some of course become sick simply because they grow older and their bodies wear out. With others there seems to be not the slightest indication that sin is the cause or is even

involved. But this area of 'confession' is one that is rarely
considered. Perhaps some leaders feel sorry for the sick
person. They wouldn't want to add to their suffering, by
adding the burden of sin to their physical ailment. But those
who call on their elders or ministers should be ready and
willing to confess sin, receive prayer and get better. The
laying on of hands is not merely symbolic. It is an impar-
tation of life, healing and the Holy Spirit.

Faith and suffering

So where are we? We in Britain are at a low level of faith.
Faith-filled churches are the exception to the rule. Sickness is
looked upon as being unfortunate, inconvenient and certainly not desirable. But a theology of sickness and 'lessons
learnt' has robbed the sick of good. 'He has sent me to
proclaim liberty to the captives and recovery of sight to the
blind; to set free the oppressed and announce that the time
has come when the Lord will save his people' (Luke 4:18–19
GNB). So why are Christians sick?

For those of us who hold to kingdom theology, faith is also
crucial to the equation. When we encounter sickness, we
must not assume it to be caused by deliberate and un-
confessed sin in the person's life – the example of Job and the
words of Jesus militate against such a simplistic view. But the
sickness can be the testing ground for faith as it is the
battleground in the battle between Satan and God. We must
realise that it is not God's will that we should be sick (except
in the permissive sense), but that the sickness provides an
opportunity to exercise greater faith in his power.

Suffering is a complex issue. No one can live in this world
without it touching our lives. Those whose aim in life is to
evade it become shallow and either retreatist or triumphalistic. Before we move on to ask, 'Where do we start?' in this
area of 'signs and wonders', we must directly address the
subject of suffering.

Sickness is to be withstood and prayed against. Suffering is
nevertheless a part of life. We cannot live in this world

without sharing and participating in its tragedies and pain. With most sickness there is pain, but there is also suffering that is experienced without sickness.

Let's look at three sides to this problem of suffering and sickness and then see how the New Testament explains it.

Three aspects

First, there is an obvious and direct connection between sickness, suffering and sin. There is what has been called the sin-suffering-repentance-restoration cycle. It is of course related to the law of sowing and reaping. Deuteronomy's list of the consequences of disobedience makes horrific reading (Deuteronomy 27; 28).

Second, as we saw in the case of Job, God obviously allows evil forces and personalities to inflict suffering and test his servants. This is primarily an Old Testament emphasis and is not noted as such in the New Testament, but the rationale that every craftsman will test his material, and creation, does have New Testament backing. 'Remember how the Lord your God led you on this long journey through the desert these past forty years, sending hardships to test you, so that he might know what you intended to do and whether you would obey his commands' (Deuteronomy 8:2 GNB). 'Endure hardship as discipline; God is treating you as sons. For what son is not disciplined by his father?' (Hebrews 12:7).

Third, and this too is a particularly Old Testament emphasis, the issue of suffering is seen in the light of the ungodly oppressor. In fact in the Old Testament there is no word which is simply translated 'suffer' or 'suffering'. Invariably the enemies (both physical and spiritual) of God's people take advantage of those who are sick. God's people often experienced national oppression.

Another dimension

In the New Testament, however, we see another aspect. There it is clearly stated that those who are not suffering are not necessarily pleasing God (Luke 6:24–25; 13:1–5; 16:19–31). Likewise there is also evidence that Jesus short-circuited the notion that those who are suffering are always wrong-doers (John 9:1–3). He did however underscore the obvious, that wrongdoing *can* cause sickness, disease and related disorders (John 5:14; cf. 1 Corinthians 11:29–30).

Again, although the people of God are no longer a national geographic entity in the New Testament, the idea remains of the innocent suffering. James attributed certain testing experiences to Satan (James 1:1–15). The writer to the Hebrew Christians paralleled certain types of suffering with a father's discipline (Hebrews 12:3–11). But the Holy Spirit is not seen as the *cause* of suffering. Indeed James makes this point clearly. 'Happy is the person who remains faithful under trials, because when he succeeds in passing such a test, he will receive as his reward the life which God has promised to those who love him. If a person is tempted by such trials, he must not say, "This temptation comes from God." For God cannot be tempted by evil, and he himself tempts no one' (James 1:12–13 GNB). God does however *allow* suffering, enabling his purposes to be realised, which is always for our good: 'For it is better to suffer for doing good, if this should be God's will, than for doing evil' (1 Peter 3:17 GNB). The New Testament also affirms that God is God, and that Satan's sphere of influence and power to inflict suffering are therefore limited and controlled by God's permissive will (Revelation 2:10).

However, all *this* suffering is within the realm of physical persecution, the demonic, or is related to the law of sowing and reaping. So when a person '*suffers*' he is to 'pray for strength and perseverance' (James 5:13–18). However, when a person is *sick*, he or she is to call for the elders, as we have seen. Their confession (if appropriate) and the elders' faith will facilitate healing.

Health and healing

Yet even the New Testament does not show us a perfect church in perfect health. Trophimus was left sick at Miletus (2 Timothy 4:20). Paul wrote to his apprentice, 'stop drinking only water, and use a little wine because of your stomach and your frequent illnesses' (1 Timothy 5:23), proving that proper care for ourselves (health) is infinitely better than healing. So whether we need prayer or better eating and drinking habits, there must be a humble but strong trust in God's word and his ways. There is nothing automatic about health or healing. We are not to use God as our servant; instead we are to serve him with humility. Prayer, faith, trust, perseverance, common sense, and compassion are all part of the divine mixture that should normally accomplish God's will in this matter.

There are many factors that hinder healing: our lack of faith, demonic opposition, psychological hang-ups on the part of those being prayed for (and those praying) or even, as is true in some cases, the enjoyment of our sickness.

The New Testament is clear. It draws a distinction between suffering, for which we need the virtues of perseverance and endurance, and the pain that is frequently experienced alongside specific sickness and illness.

Living in the fallen world in which we do, suffering is inevitable. A broken friendship, bereavement, financial losses, national disasters, are often beyond our control. They are also beyond our faith. Indeed Jesus warned that there would be wars, famines and the such before he returned. We must pray that in such situations, so often caused by man's stupidity and inhumanity, the love and mercy of God will break through. Some suffering may be avoided through prayer and living responsibly, but by no means all.

All sickness, on the other hand, is to be resisted, rejected and prayed against. God intends to grow our faith, to strengthen it and effect change in circumstances of human misery and pain experienced through sickness.

What next?

Having assessed our present position with regard to the world, health, faith, sickness and suffering, the next step is crucial. If there really is a 'better way', as we saw in the last chapter, how do we bridge the gap between the reality of our present position and where we would like to be?

WHERE DO WE START?

The only difference between lives of aspiration and achievement is development. How can we develop faith? What can we do to see signs and wonders follow our ministry and lifestyle? What pitfalls can we avoid as we launch out into an area that is regarded as being a minefield?

Acknowledge that there is no blueprint

In scripture God provides principles and guidelines to help us live our Christian lives. But he also leaves a measure of uncertainty over some issues so that we will be dependent on his Holy Spirit for guidance. The important thing to be aware of is that God's word does not always provide a blueprint outlining exactly how we are to approach a task. The area of signs and wonders is just such a case. Here Jesus is our prime example, as in so many areas of life. But when we see how he dealt with the demonised and the sick, it is clear that he treated different situations with different techniques. For those of us who want a scriptural 'user's manual' we are liable to be very disappointed at his lack of a consistent method: sometimes he healed with a word, sometimes a touch.

In this whole area it is vital that we honour those who are experienced in signs and wonders and healings. We will of course want to follow Jesus' example and teaching, but another aspect of Christian discipleship is that we can learn from other Christians. We must never merely imitate them; what may 'work' for them may not work for us. So we have to exercise discernment. That is important because there are two traps we can fall into here.

First, we can idolise God's servants. The danger here is not one that only affects us who idolise; it also affects those we idolise and put on a pedestal. Our adulation can harm those we admire. Many good leaders have been compromised or even had their ministries ruined by the sins of greed (the love of money), lust (the lures of sex) and feelings of increasing independence and personal power (the foolishness of pride) – all of which can be fuelled by our lack of care in this matter. We must pray that here in Britain our leaders may be saved from such dangers.

Second, we can criticise the faults and failings of such people. We may not like the way they do things. Or their style may irritate us. So we get to work with our deadly tongues. It's like stabbing them in the back, but without the need to actually get that close and plunge the knife in for ourselves. We just venture our opinions and let things go from there. They are too noisy, we say. They are too quiet. They are not specific enough in their definitions of medical conditions so there's bound to be someone who thinks they are being referred to. They play to the gallery . . . and so on.

The issue here is ultimately one of honour, not style and personal preference. Honour has to do with a person's dignity, value and worth, both as a person and in terms of their ministry. Our critical tongue-wagging dishonours God's servants, although of course 'That's not what we intended to do' – we were just offering a point of view. The trouble is, there are two victims: whenever we dishonour others in this way we also dishonour ourselves.

Learn to listen

'Faith comes from hearing the message, and the message comes through preaching Christ' (Romans 10:17 GNB). If that faith is to grow we must develop the ability to listen, respond and listen again. There are various ways in which God speaks, so we must keep a listening ear in all of them.

Firstly and most importantly, God speaks through scripture. Here we see the heroes of faith, and there are many lessons to be learnt from their lives and teaching.

Secondly, John (Jesus' best friend) called him the Word of God (John 1:1–18). Thank God for words, but Christ by his Spirit is still wanting to speak to us today. This is somewhat subjective, so anything of a directive nature needs checking out with others. But Jesus, who is the Word, hasn't spoken his last word.

Thirdly, we must listen to those around us. Christians who are obviously growing in faith and devotion to Christ can only inspire and strengthen us. But we must also listen to those who do not share our faith. We are very good at answering questions nobody is asking. Our faith will become more relevant to others if we listen to them and 'scratch where they are itching'.

Deal with recurring negativism

I have rarely known God powerfully use a negative person. We must abhor pessimism. G. K. Chesterton once said, 'Show me a pessimist, and I will show you a man who has never suffered.' Only the man who has suffered somewhat can afford to be optimistic. Optimism must not be confused with faith, but pessimism is no platform for faith.

Those in leadership should be providing a helpful environment for individuals to pray, speak in tongues and interpret, heal the sick and cast out demons. We never flourish under constant disapproval. We all grow when encouraged, even when we know that we may not have done that well.

But leaders are not the only ones who ought to encourage and approve of people and their gifts. Simply to say to someone, 'I was so helped by your prophecy' is a sign of positive acceptance of their ministry. We should wonder why it doesn't happen more often. Signs and wonders indeed!

A great deal of faithless depression stems from self-imposed negative thinking. But thinking and speaking are closely related. Jesus is the high priest of our confession. 'Your words will be used to judge you – to declare you either innocent or guilty' (Matthew 12:37 GNB). We often overstate our difficulties and undervalue ourselves. We get locked into fearful and bothersome perspectives that leave hardly any room for hope. Criticising the successes and gifts of others soon follows on. And, as we have just seen, that has dangers all of its own.

Finding faith does not go hand in hand with recurring negativism. Negative attitudes lead to pride and wanting to be right. Instead, humble yourself, confess your sin and apologise to those you may have wronged or hurt. God will give you grace and in time a whole new way to live. Trying to work up a positive outlook is not the antidote to negativism. The road of apology is.

Be specific

'If you believe, you will receive whatever you ask for in prayer' (Matthew 21:22). Consciously or unconsciously, many people avoid disappointment by not being specific in their prayers. 'If you don't ask specifically, you don't end up with specific egg on your face,' a friend told me recently.

But asking God generally to bless so and so, or this and that is unquantifiable. 'God bless London' is difficult to measure in grateful thanks or testimony. But ask God for an act, a specific situation, and that is a different matter.

I was once included in a major evangelistic initiative in London. The BBC filmed the meetings, the speaker and the converts. Unfortunately the vehicle containing their equipment and all the cans of film was stolen. I wanted to pray very specifically that we would get the films back. That night a senior organiser asked me to explain the situation to several thousand in the meeting and pray for the return of the van and its contents.

The next day I went to Germany to speak at some meetings. Upon my return, I was told, 'You are in trouble with the BBC!' It turned out that the thief had come back to the meeting stadium to return all the cans of unedited film. But the equipment and BBC vehicle were never seen again!

A basic principle of physics is that it is easier to redirect a moving object. If we are moving in prayer and we make specific requests, we will occasionally get things wrong. But when things are moving we can examine our attitude of heart, chalk up our failures to experience, get up and get on with it. God doesn't get disillusioned with us, he never had any illusions in the first place! Our failures should make us dependent on God, with a desire to know his mind, heart and plans.

Declare War!

When people give their lives to Christ they change sides and realign their allegiances. Every believer is in a war. Our beliefs, prayers and actions are to take ground from Satan and give it back to God. In out and out war there is no demilitarised zone. The overall campaign and individual battles involve identifying the enemy, responding to commands from our superior and coming against the enemy with weapons we have been given.

If a person is demonised it is useless praying, 'Lord help the demons to go' or, 'We ask that these demons will leave our friend at sometime or another'! That is not how to conduct a battle.

My first 'deliverance' involved a girl who was afraid of God, the devil, the dark, men and just about anything else you care to mention. With another person (the girl's present friend), I closed my eyes, reminded her of Jesus' love and then asked her if she wanted to be free from this paralysing fear. 'Oh yes please,' she replied. I began to pray quietly for her: 'Then in Jesus' name . . .' – but before I could continue she let out an awful agonised scream. I looked up. To my horror I saw that this otherwise quiet teenager had leapt out of her seat and with fingers aimed at my eyes was about to descend on me! I lifted myself out of my seat, challenged this enemy within her in tongues (I couldn't think of anything else to say) and shouted, 'Out!' With that, the girl slumped back into her chair, to the astonishment of her friend. I was so nervous I was almost in a state of shock. But I tried to play the part of the professional however. 'Are you OK Louise?' I asked hesitantly. 'Oh yes, I'm fine now,' she replied, with the colour coming back to her face. I tried to joke: 'You should have seen your face,' I chuckled. 'You should have seen yours!' she replied hilariously!

It has been said that Satan only troubles those who trouble him. Usually there are less dramatic reasons why people have fears. Most fearful people just need a good dose of God's love. Prayer, counsel and friendships are the usual course for wholeness and stability. But even they must be seen in terms of a love that outdoes enemy fear, and a truth that exposes Satanic lies. Confrontation of the sort I had with Louise and her friend is the bottom line, not the first course of action. Only a few very experienced leaders and people with specific ministries will know in moments whether a person needs deliverance of this sort. Remember, however, it is the name of Jesus and the power of his Spirit that gives us success, not our voice-level, our charismatic personalities or our superior knowledge.

In the spiritual battle we are not to abandon our critical faculties. What we must do is employ them all, with humble dependence on God. This way our aspirations will be turned to achievements. In war it is our job to restrict Satan's activity, at the very least!

Make room for others

Jesus is our prophet, priest and king, but he is also apostle, evangelist, healer, deliverer, teacher, pastor and much more. Now the church has people who are apostles, evangelists and the like.

I would like to be able to preach the gospel, plant churches, pastor the sheep, open up the scriptures, heal the sick, deliver the demonised and generally be everything to everybody. However, I don't have the same gifting or humility as Jesus. With respect, I also have to say that he was the first of his kind. He had no church, fellowship or highly trained and experienced body of people around him. His disciples were a wonderful bunch, but they didn't know what was happening

half the time! Jesus had to do it all, at least until they were
ready to practise some of the gifts themselves.

It is right to pray to Jesus, the head of the church (Col-
ossians 1:18), but often in our everyday tasks it is not just the
head we need but also the body. We are the 'many-
membered body of Christ'. Jesus could be in only one place;
today we are everywhere. This is how he wanted it. Today,
via the gifts he showers upon us, he works through *us* –
everywhere.

But how do we work together as Christ's body? How does
the fact that we need each other work out in practice? Well,
one may have a burden to see God do something – but he or
she may not know what to do with that burden. Another may
have insights into a situation while another may know how to
pray specifically for it. Such prayer may be for healing or
deliverance.

Only a few carry great burdens, have remarkable insights
and know how to pray at all times. Most of us don't. That is
why I am a great believer in teams. Teamwork is a welcome
emphasis to those of us who have done everything on our own
– from hauling out the hymnbooks to casting out demons.

Teams provide some safeguards as well. I don't allow men
in the churches we care for to counsel women on their own.
They have to have at least one other person present, prefer-
ably their wife. The same principle applies to women counselling men. A strange mixture of genuine desire to help and
other less helpful factors can come into an intense counselling relationship. Also the presence of the third person can
help enormously if the counsellor is not able to see all the
issues clearly.

In an age of independence and a 'no one is going to tell me
what to do' philosophy, we must pray for an undying sense of
a need of one another. The answer to the one-man ministry is
not the everyman ministry in which everybody – instead of
the one man – tries to do everything. Complementarity is
what it's all about. Different people's gifts and abilities inter-
mesh and work together.

We may at times need to fast *together* rather than on our

own. We can do this as a small group or even as a church.
Going without food and praying instead – in faith and with
friends – sharpens our spiritual perceptions. We should
expect God to speak to us. Then we can submit any guidance
to responsible people to test whether or not our 'leading' or
'insights' are from God. In relationship there is safety,
wisdom and generally a higher degree of success and
blessing. There is joy and power in doing things *together* for
God.

Raise your level of faith

All of the things I have just mentioned should help to raise
our level of faith – but we must make growth in faith a specific
priority. The person who has never had to believe that God
can provide the money for a bus fare or car repair bill is
unlikely to be able to trust God for £100,000 for property.
The one who has never believed God for healing in minor
illnesses (aching backs, imperfect hearing, or sight) will be
unlikely to see people leap out of wheelchairs as a result of
prayer.

Ask any healing evangelist and they will tell you that there
is a low level of faith in Britain. Well-known, mature,
overseas evangelists who see lots of 'signs and wonders' in
many other countries do not see much more happen here
than we do through our own local ministries.

Yet many younger and less experienced Christians do not
have such a problem with faith. Perhaps they are not as
'sophisticated', 'knowledgeable' and 'rational' as us. For
instance, a colleague came back from a meeting and told his
wife and eighteen year old son, 'Cor – we saw God heal three
sick people and deliver two demonised people in the meeting
tonight. It was wonderful!' His son replied, 'Oh come off it,
Dad, we see that sort of thing happen every week in our youth
meeting!'

My own faith has also been challenged in a similar way.
Two of our three sons used to share a bedroom. One evening
Paul, our eldest, came in covered in lumps and weals. They

were in every conceivable place. Since there was no apparent reason for this condition, my wife wanted to call the doctor, but Simon, our second child, rebuked her. 'What about prayer then?' he demanded.

When I arrived home it was my job to steer Simon in his praying. Not the most sophisticated of teenagers, he said 'Lord – Paul looks horrible. Make him better. Amen!' I paused and in the silence prayed, 'Lord, you know Simon's a novice in all this – he doesn't know how to pray, but his heart is right, so if you can arrange to answer his prayer it would be rather nice.'

The next morning as Anona (my wife) and I sat in bed having coffee, 'They're goooooooooone!' rang through the house. I immediately thought that the goldfish must have jumped out of their bowl! We ran into the room, and there was Paul with not a mark on him and Simon with a proud grin from ear to ear! All I knew was that it was not my prayer that had made Paul well – it was Simon's. To him there had been no problem, yet my attitude had been to assume I knew best what sort of prayer God wanted to hear.

'Unless you change and become like little children . . .' our Lord said (Matthew 18:3). We all want to be so grown up – that's our problem. We want to understand sickness. We read books on it and watch television programmes on the subject. Yet even so-called charismatic believers have only got to get a headache or the sniffles and they are off to the doctor. Only after that, if the pills, potions and creams haven't worked, do we turn to prayer. There is of course nothing wrong with medication, it is a matter of where our trust is. Our trust must be in the Lord, not in his servants or in the medical profession as such. 'Some patients feel we can't make mistakes and that we can heal anybody of almost anything,' a doctor told me. 'We can't heal anything. We can deal with the symptoms or remove offending organs, but that's it,' he continued. 'We are doctors, not healers,' he said.

We should never get our values upside down. It is fine to take appropriate action. So if I have a headache I quickly take a tablet to enable me to get on with my work without distraction. We should never feel guilty about that. But our trust must never be allowed to rest in our GP or our local hospitals.

Cynicism and faith

Our faith will never grow if we surround ourselves with cynics, whose tendency in life is to disbelieve. There is a difference between questioning things (as we are encouraged to do by scripture) and having as our aim in life the diminishing and, if possible, the disproving of the unexplainable and irrational. This tendency to disbelieve is rife. It even manifests itself in healing meetings.

For example, if you say to a thousand people, 'There is someone here with a bad back,' that is not a word of knowledge or even discernment. With forty per cent of the adult population suffering from back problems, one would need a word of knowledge to say, 'No one here has a back problem!' But I have heard speakers say something as specific and clear as this: 'There is someone here, a woman who fell off a ladder this week. She has injured her shoulder, damaged her left leg and was almost stopped coming to the meeting tonight by her sister.' But such is the tendency to disbelieve that the person in question looks around and behind to see if anyone else fits into that category!

There are several positive things we can do to increase our faith and resist the pall of cynicism. Read scripture and pray whenever you feel like it, and even at times when you don't. Nurture friendships with those whose faith in God is growing. Let the cynics be challenged by the faith of you and your friends or let them stew in their own poisonous cynicism. They suffer from a 'hardening of attitudes', but you mustn't. Ask God to keep your heart tender towards himself and those around you. It will hurt at times, but it's worth it because Jesus is worth it. Faith will rise in God's ability, and if you become properly disillusioned with your own abilities, you will be asking God to surprise you – continually! Repent of unbelief, learn to handle mistakes, apologise where necessary, and live in the tension of bringing the next age into this one.

Taking the steps outlined in this chapter will help us to bridge the gap between the poles of aspiration and achievement that we noted earlier on.

There are various tensions that we are exposed to in the Christian life. We have noted several, perhaps the most important being that between faith and unbelief. But there is also a proper tension between the ideal and the actual. Derek Prince once said that maturity involves aiming for the ideal while we learn to live with the actual. Immaturity is, on the other hand, evidenced by either living entirely with the actual and losing all sight of the ideal or refusing to accept the actual and constantly chasing after the ideal as if that alone mattered. Ultimately Jesus was the only person who could successfully resolve that tension, and he gave his life in order to do so. To those of us who long to see God move in power, for his glory, that is good news: our success does not depend on our efforts but on what our Lord has achieved for us!

IT'S GOOD NEWS!

It is not enough for Christ's church to *have* good news – we must also *be* good news. At present the church in Britain *has* good news but *is* by and large bad news. You can help change that. How do we get from here to there then? Many wish they were in different churches, another environment with a different set of friends. That is a dangerous attitude. Comparison – another factor destructive to faith – takes over and makes everything seem futile.

One day a friend of mine got lost in London. He parked his car, leaned out of the window, stopped a passer-by and asked how he could get to his destination. The pedestrian looked around, put his computer-like brain into gear and replied, 'I am sorry – I don't think you can get there from here!' My colleague was almost speechless. 'But this is where I am,' he blurted out. 'I can't start from anywhere else – this is where I am. Even if I've got to start somewhere else, I must be able to get *there* from here, because I can't start anywhere else!'

It is important we learn from that logic. It was ridiculous to say my friend couldn't get to where he wanted from where he was. You as an individual and we as a church *can* close the gap between what we say we believe and how we live. The good news is that we *can* get to where we want from where we are!

But our good news must be communicated *as* good news. Our role as believers is to make Jesus 'visible, desirable and understandable.' For sinners, the good news is forgiveness. For the sick, the good news is a God who heals. For the poor, the good news is the redistribution of resources (a highfalutin way of saying we share what we have with those who have virtually nothing).

Let's think about them all in turn.

Sinners and forgiveness

To preachers I say, Let's talk about the good news in a good fashion. We can make good news sound terribly bad!

God does not want unbelievers making an unreasonable commitment based on inadequate evidence. We may often be the only initial evidence people have of Christ and his gospel. We get things mixed up if we think that our role as sharers, teachers and preachers of the gospel is to make the guilty feel guilty. Rather, we are to point out God's demands and show how wonderful Jesus was and is in dying and now living for us.

We need passion in the pulpit again. We are to humbly serve this gospel of good news – we are not to get it to serve us! Scripture, history and our own personal stories blend into one – to declare to those who feel cut off from God that 'There is forgiveness and reconciliation.' If we view God as a disapproving moral watchdog, we will communicate such a God – whatever words we use.

We know that the good news is central in Christ dying on our behalf for all the wrongs we have done. He was punished in our place. But the good news goes on to declare that he rose from the grave, is alive today and loves the wrongdoer but hates the wrong done. The good news is that the dying saviour is our living saviour. 'If Christ has not been raised from death, then we have nothing to preach and you have nothing to believe' (1 Corinthians 15:14 GNB).

His love is alive, for God is alive: willing, waiting and wanting to extend forgiveness to every repentant wrongdoer. Our God is one of mercy, compassion and forgiveness. It is often the overwhelming sense of God's love for us that leads sinners to a change of heart.

Wrong must be pointed out. Calvary stands as God's statement towards sin and wrongdoing. But the penalty has been met. The punishment has fitted the crimes. To all who believe the gospel story and put their trust in Jesus there is forgiveness and eternal life.

The sick and healing

Jesus' ministry was heralded by 'peace' from the angels (Luke 2:14). When Christ visited his disciples in the upper room, he said 'peace' (Luke 24:36; John 20:21). We often want to start with power, dynamite and miracles, but all these are to bring joy and peace to people.

Peace brings healing – to our emotions, to our relationships, to our minds and to our bodies. Being at peace with God should lead us to healing power. Peace comes when we cease to resist his will for our lives.

This source of healing is in Christ. One day a colleague of mine who had been married for less than two years came home to find his wife dead on the kitchen floor. Leukaemia had claimed another victim. Many years later his teenage son was diagnosed as having cancer. He was miraculously healed – and today, several years later, remains so. My colleague would say that both he and his church had grown in faith. He said recently at a leaders' meeting, 'We lost the first battle, but we went on to win the second.' Even in his loss he found peace with God and went on to power.

The church remains sick – the world gets sicker. So we need to ask some questions. Do we want to manage the mess or stop the mess wherever we can? Do we want to be nibbled to death by sectional interests or by fear of making mistakes, or do we want to reverse things by putting our faith in God? This is where our previous theme of 'battle' re-enters our discussion.

Part of our trouble is that we do not see ourselves as a persecuted minority. 'Battle?' says the average Christian, 'What battle?' Well for a start we have the enemy of sickness and disease among us. Take that healing out on to the streets and those prayed for will become friends and colleagues in arms. Our willingness to pray for people must be personal, practical and perennial. The good news is that you care enough to pray. In so doing you give people back a sense of dignity and self-respect. You also give those you are praying for the privilege of exercising faith and God is given the opportunity to act. The more we pray for each other the more God has an opportunity to demonstrate his healing power among us.

The poor and resources

When believers give to one another in a glad and sacrificial manner, they offer a sign of God's grace and presence. In an age of 'get-as-much-as-you-can-as-quick-as-you-can' it will certainly get people looking on in wonder.

Walking in the hills of Sweden, one day, I was told by God to give my car to a friend who had no vehicle. It was my first brand-new automobile – a black John Player Special Capri. I had no money for another car. Two weeks later I handed over the keys and the car to an astonished fellow leader! His parents enquired what he was doing driving around in my car. 'He's given it to me,' he told them, still somewhat incredulously. 'Why? What's wrong with it?' they asked. That sums up people's attitudes so often. They found it impossible to believe he should be given the car for nothing.

On another occasion an international personality came to stay with us to speak at several meetings. As a church we wanted to bless him. We gave him £300 within a day or so of his arrival. 'What's this for?' he asked. 'It's for you,' I said on behalf of my leadership team. 'There will be offerings for your work in the meetings, but this is for you and your wife, simply to help you have a pleasant stay.' I left the room. Unknown to me at that time, he had given all his money away and had been badly used by unscrupulous individuals. He came to Britain with an international name and £5 in his pocket. Later he wept and said, 'This is the first time I have been given something for nothing. People always give me things because they want something out of me!' This sharing of resources left an incredible impression on us both.

Generosity has not always marked the church and is certainly not the hallmark of evangelicalism. 'And what are your expenses?' asks the treasurer. As he probably knows where the speaker lives and how many miles he has travelled he could easily assess that. But making a gift on the basis of totalling up miles per gallon is embarrassing and doesn't take into account car depreciation, time of preparation, mortgage, and so on. The hallmark of the early church was generosity, blessing and caring extravagance.

A group that meets each other's needs in a loving and caring way can be a wonderful backdrop to a more dramatic 'miraculous' ministry. After a particularly bad FA cup final, a senior FA official asked the Queen, 'Did you feel anybody played particularly well, Ma'am?' She replied somewhat drily, 'The band – just the band.' As a church, our attitude to money can be a bit like that. The prelude to sacrificial love (preaching about it) is often better than the actual game (living it).

We mustn't wait for central initiatives from the PCC, the deacons or the elders. We can be the first to take a chance and make it happen, the first to see a need and endeavour to meet it. We can take a chance and do something. Unfortunately it was and still is respectable to do nothing. Fulfilment for the Christian is never found in accumulating money and resources but in humble obedience to demonstrate practical love to those around us.

Our God-ordained policy is to prefer our brothers over and above ourselves. Large homes that are filled with many things and accompanied by holidays in far-away places are only legitimate provided they are not goals. The soul of service is care, and by the resources he has given us God gives you and me the opportunity of showing we care. Older believers have to ask not so much, 'What shall I do if I don't reach my goals in life?' but rather, 'What shall I do if I do?'

We should all be aware of needs in our own churches and fellowships and be ready to meet them. The poor, elderly, unemployed and sick need special, sensitive attention. It may be that we bring the need to our minister or elders so that central funds can meet that need. On the other hand we should be open to meet that need out of our own personal resources.

I took a small team to South Africa recently and carried collections from many individuals and churches. We shared that money with leaders in struggling situations and the poor blacks in the townships. Many wept as they were given food, clothes and money. We explained we represented the living God and that he is on the side of the poor and what sociologists call 'the marginals' of society. The response (not that we looked for one) was wonderful.

There are many other things we could say about blessing the poor, both personally and through the churches. Little is actually addressed to the poor in scripture, but much to those who are in a position to be 'good news' to the poor. It is not just the church leader's job, or even the government's, to care for such groups: we all have a responsibility to pray, care and give.

Renewal, restoration or a revival will quietly evaporate if we do not allow God to touch our wallets, purses and bank accounts.

Visible daily signs

There are far too many in the church who are not living in God's forgiveness, health, or resources. For some the blame may lie clearly on their doorstep – for others it may lie with us. We dare not presume that the ill-fortune of others is invariably their own fault. If we are sensitive to those less fortunate than ourselves, God will display through this sign the wonders of his grace and power. It was Blaise Pascal who quite brilliantly wrote:

> 'It is vain O man
> That you seek within yourself
> The cure for your miseries.
> Your principle maladies
> Are pride, which cuts you off from God

> And sensuality which binds you to the earth.
> Either you imagine you are gods yourselves.
> Or you grasp the vanity of the situation
> And you are cast into the other abyss.
> And suppose yourselves to be
> The beasts of the field, and
> Seek your good through sensual appetites.'

These remarkable words are for us, God's people, as well as the unconverted. Humanity can be both the glory and the rubbish of the universe. When we become like gods, we are on a course of selfish pride. When we sink into bestiality we lose all self respect. Both courses make rubbish of our dignified humanity. But where we see the sharing of resources, the love of God for all people demonstrated so tangibly, there we see God's glory.

When I was seventeen years old, I borrowed a friend's motorbike. Without my friend's permission, a crash helmet, a licence or insurance, I set off. Within minutes I had to negotiate a difficult situation. I failed. One week later I came round, and remained semi-conscious for another week. My skull, back and ribs were all fractured, one eye was blinded, five clots of blood lodged around my brain and I was initially expected to live for only four hours. I still have the medical sheet my parents were given which sent them home to wait for me to die that night.

My friends prayed against all odds that I would survive. One close friend, who was backslidden at the time, when he heard the news that night, put his drink down, went home, knelt by his bed and came back to Christ. Others continued in prayer until I was well. We need to 'continue in prayer' and not give up after the first go! Perhaps if they had, I wouldn't be here today. There are forces at work that would have liked my voice to be silenced and my life to be extinguished. So it is with you.

The greatest sign

I appreciate that love, prayers and sacrificial giving are not virtues exclusive to the Christian faith. But *our* love stems from God's love. Our prayers are met not by a stone idol of a bygone age, but a living God who is touched by our dilemmas and painful predicaments. Our model is Jesus, who loved us and gave himself for us while we were still 'in our sins'. What a God! What a saviour! What a sign!

We must never forget that a changed life is the greatest sign that causes most to wonder. This phrase 'signs and wonders' must not be boxed and restricted into healing, deliverance and the gifts of the Spirit. All 'signs and wonders' cause God to be glorified in changed hearts, renewed minds, healed bodies and mended relationships.

It is Jesus – the greatest sign and wonder, who did so many signs and wonders – who makes changed lives possible.

Triumph and triumphalism

Jesus' disciples found that when his power had been transferred, they became channels of the miraculous. They returned from their mission not only in triumph but somewhat triumphalistic. They were suddenly aware that Caesar didn't control all things and that the Pharisees didn't control people from the inside. Their obedience to Jesus and belief in his teaching, coupled with their confidence in the Spirit, reversed the trend of things. They saw that the word of God had power.

But miraculously changing matter (sickness giving way to health) and seeing dark powers flee, is heady stuff. So Jesus said, 'Listen! I have given you authority, so that you can walk on snakes and scorpions and overcome all the power of the Enemy, and nothing will hurt you. But don't be glad because the evil spirits obey you; rather be glad because your names are written in heaven' (Luke 10:19–20 GNB). He didn't slap them down with the three marks of conservative evangelicalism: cynicism, pessimism and criticism. Jesus was

thrilled in his soul with what they had done, as the following
verses allow us to see: '"Father, Lord of heaven and earth! I
thank you because you have shown to the unlearned what
you have hidden from the wise and learned. Yes, Father, this
was how you wanted it to happen." Then Jesus turned to the
disciples and said to them privately, "How fortunate you are
to see the things you see! I tell you that many prophets and
kings wanted to see what you see, but they could not, and to
hear what you hear, but they did not"' (Luke 10:21–24).

No wonder those early disciples were excited. They probably were not fully aware of what was taking place, but the
age to come was breaking in on the present age.

Jesus is committed to doing the same sort of thing today.
He is committed to his people. 'Covenant [an agreement] is
abandoning the right to quit,' says David Sheppard. Jesus
has abandoned the right to quit from redeeming the earth
until 'the earth will be as full of the knowledge of the Lord's
glory as the seas are full of water' (Habakkuk 2:14).

If God's blessing causes excitement it dare not be damp-
ened. It may need gentle redirection.

Getting the scene

William Booth once said, 'We cannot change the future
without disturbing the present.' The current emphasis on
relationships, shepherding, discipleship and community
bears witness to this. The stage is being set for Jesus to mend
the church wherever he is allowed to exercise his power. Such
relationships of love and care allow emotional healing as well
as reconciliation and are surely a welcome background for
the proclamation of the kingdom in power.

Generally speaking, people become emotionally sick when
they respond to situations in an unbiblical manner. A small
percentage of emotional illness is directly related to brain
damage or chemical imbalances – especially in the thyroid
gland. But by far the major reason for such emotional illness
is when we turn what could be building bricks into stumbling
blocks. Everything in life, all losses as well as gains, can

either become building bricks into life's experience or stumbling blocks over which we fall and damage ourselves.

We may lose a friend, see a plan fail dismally or find ourselves in circumstances beyond our control. How are we to react? Do we shrug our shoulders, invite God to make sense of it all, put our faith in him and carry on with life? Do we ask God's forgiveness for any areas of unhealthy anger, resentment and self-pity? Or do we adopt a 'life's not fair' attitude and nurture the idea that God and those around us owe us something?

It is sometimes difficult to detect which category people are in when they live in one town, work in another and worship in yet another. That is why I feel that God welcomes the increasing emphasis on the church being local. It creates more opportunities for friendship, health, wholeness and healing at every level. People can be better helped, blessed and equipped for action. This action will first take place locally, then in a wider area and then in the whole world. The church is to be a sort of community in each locality, and those outside of that community are supposed to be challenged and have their consciences pricked by the evident love, care and interest members of the body of Christ show one to another. Of course in the final analysis all of that love and care must burst out of the constraints of church life into the whole of society.

Many areas within towns and cities need Christians to either move in and *be* a church or, if they are already there, to stop commuting elsewhere. This is true for many villages as well. Large churches should release resources to be good news wherever people live. It was David Pawson who said, 'Your road should be a better place to live because you live there.' Those on the outside of church life should be able to see believers living and worshipping together. They have a right to see how Christ has enabled people to live together in harmony, not travel to church together with no strategy.

God's plan is that his good news should, wherever possible, be 'good newsed' by people living, worshipping and – if possible – working in the same area. With clear channels of communication and daily opportunity, the people of God can be far more effective in their witness than the 'church on wheels' each Sunday.

We shall be able to help the poor in our locality and pray for the sick among our circle of working relationships and friendships. Then our good news will not be hidden, but will shine brightly.

BACK TO THE FUTURE!

Sins and blunders must give way to signs and wonders! Instead of wanting us to have a jaundiced view of eschatology (future events), God stands ready to fill us with faith. Instead of smallness and failure, God is preparing the church for greatness. True; 'in the last days difficult times will come. For men will be lovers of self, lovers of money, boastful, arrogant, revilers, disobedient to parents, ungrateful, unholy, unloving, irreconcilable, malicious gossips, without self-control, brutal, haters of good, treacherous, reckless, conceited, lovers of pleasure rather than lovers of God' (2 Timothy 3:1–4 NASB), but Jesus made a difference. His first disciples made a difference. Those people throughout history most devoted to Jesus and the scriptures have made a difference.

We must look beyond the present. 'Give us ten years,' I often tell our critics, 'and by God's grace we'll make a difference!' We must keep a heavenly perspective. For alongside tribulation and a falling away in certain quarters, revival and church growth are taking place all across the world. While it is true that more people have been martyred this century than in all the others put together, the light of Christ is shining brightly and God's people are growing in Third World countries. Heroes of faith abound in Russia, China, South America, Korea, the Philippines and in many other areas. Despite hurt, injury, ridicule, opposition and persecution, our future is optimistic.

Glorious simplicity

P. G. Johnston, who compiled various facts and figures in his book *Operation World*, clearly underlines this view. He reasons

that the pessimism of believers in the West regarding the
decline in Christian faith and morality is not based on
reality. Progress is slow and the good news is not always
carried with the sensational activity of our enemy. But
worldwide the church is understanding that Christ is a
universal man. A man for all nations, all colours, all cultures.
Without the worldly sophistication of the west, Third World
nations are taking scripture at almost face value. 'Because of
our sins, he was wounded, beaten because of the evil we did.
We are *healed* by the punishment he suffered, *made whole* by
the blows he received' (Isaiah 53:5 GNB). Healing and wholeness must mark the church if she is to be effective.

We in the West must cleanse ourselves of cynicism, pessimism and criticism. We must be encouraged wherever we
hear of God at work, nationally or internationally. We must
short-circuit our 'failure syndrome' and its attendant low
level of faith. We must learn from the past so as to plan for
our future and our children's future. The rule of the church
must never be allowed to be a susbstitute for the rule of God.

We must not be surprised when wheat and tares grow up
together. God will not always vindicate us when we would
like him to. Until then, we must reflect in all we say and do an
increasing capacity for usefulness and responsibility. Then
we must let God do what only he can do. Then, when he does,
we must stand back, satisfied in part but never taking God's
glory. As Keith Green sang, 'Help me to remember, when
I'm doing well, to never take a crown.' Tares will be seen for
what they are. Humanism, hedonism, atheism, spiritism and
communism have had plenty of time to prove their point.
Through them God proves his.

A future together!

An incorrect view of Christ's purposes and second coming
can postpone God's intentions for his church. So let's start
where we are. 'Little platoons,' wrote the nineteenth-century
political observer Edmund Burke, 'are the only hope for
reshaping the morality and conscience of a country. They

will accomplish far more than the heavyweights of local or national government'. Let's ask God to increase our level of faith in his ability, and let's 'Go for it!'

There is bound to be failure because *we* are failures. Mistakes will be made. Some will exaggerate the Spirit's work, others will become triumphalistic. But we must talk truthfully and lovingly point one another to eternal values. They put our physical ones into perspective. We must not become cast adrift from what scripture teaches on this subject. Therefore we must realise that not every experience which causes us to shake or react in unusual ways is from God. That is why mature, faith-filled but level-headed leadership is needed. Nor can we legislate away the ill-motivated or the immature. Likewise, we should be aware that deliverance from the one-man ministry does tend to open us up to 'everyman' ministry. The one-man ministry is safe, but allowing people to find their own way is risky. Nevertheless, we must give up our safe areas and step out on to the danger line. But we must never throw away our critical faculties.

This does not, however, mean that we should employ our minds in a cynical fashion. There are those today, just as there were in Jesus' time, who are cynical when it comes to healing, deliverance and the miraculous. I once sat in the study of an internationally known speaker, where he challenged me with, 'Show me a miracle'. To reduce the gracious, spontaneous and merciful acts of God down to some sort of exhibition is quite despicable. Jesus refused to give signs to those who were full of unbelief and cynicism (Matthew 12:38–42). Even when somebody is genuinely healed, or their lives have been changed, it is amazing how many Christian leaders and even those who hold office in the church are keen to put it down to anything else other than God himself. A strange state of affairs.

The kingdom that Jesus taught about is 'already but not yet'. It is already here, in power, but not yet here in all its glory. Living in the fallen world in which we do, we do not have all the kingdom all the time. But for the church in Britain the issue is a clear one. How much of the age to come are we going to allow God to bring into this present age? We cannot manufacture his presence, his signs or his wonders. So while we look forward to that day when the whole of creation will be set free for all time, when every knee will bow and every tongue will confess that Jesus Christ is Lord, we must continue to pray that God's kingdom will come, and his will be done on earth as it is in heaven. The kingdom is not an ideal to be aimed at but a reality to be lived in.

Jesus broke in to the fallenness of his creation conveying God's benevolent intentions for the world. But we also have an enemy who is out to steal, kill and destroy. We are as children in an evil world. We stand cleansed by Christ amidst gross impurity. We are being straightened by the Spirit and by scripture, while surrounded by crookedness, devious behaviour and hypocrisy. Physical, emotional and spiritual breakdown and chaos are on every hand, so we need to come to terms with our present condition but also to aim for something morally, prayerfully and miraculously better.

We must remember that Israel's God of two thousand years ago is also the living God of Britain today. He stands ready and willing to extend his mercy and power in signs and wonders to his people. As we devote ourselves to God's pleasure it will involve a great deal of sacrifice, inconvenience and suffering. But what joy will be ours when alongside our hard work, determination, acts of good will and discipline God comes among us with signs and wonders. He longs to show us that he is still on the throne, that his intentions toward us are good and that he is indeed the God who is the same yesterday, today and forever.

In the age to come there will be no more sickness, no more disease, no more tears and no more darkness. But until then we should be thankful that we have a God who has left us not only a written and orderly account of how we are supposed to live but also, in the power of his Spirit, is still a God who 'gives us signs' – of his love, his power, his care and his original intentions for humankind. What a God!

He Brings Us Together

Clive Calver

He Brings Us Together traces the roots of evangelical belief and practice, sketches a short history of the movement to the present day, and calls for allegiance to the Bible and a commitment to social action and unity. This book is designed to encourage evangelicals to recognise their identity, their distinctiveness and their common ground with one another across the denominational spectrum.

He Guides Us

Jonathan Lamb

He Guides Us affirms that God does guide the lives of individual Christians precisely and effectively. At the heart of the subject of guidance lies the greatest privilege – knowing God.

This book discusses *how* God guides: through the Bible, fellow Christians, circumstances, gifts, prophecy, dreams and visions. It provides valuable help in discerning God's will and identifying his voice.

He Tells Us To Go

Ian Coffey

Ian Coffey sets out to define what evangelism really means: who it is aimed at, what the Bible says, and leaves unsaid. He asks whether this highly emotive and often misunderstood subject is a twentieth-century phenomenon of mass meetings, or a strictly one-to-one affair. *He Tells Us To Go* also discusses the relationship of evangelism to social action, to the ecumenical movement, and to other religions.

Gets to grips with awkward questions. A very helpful little booklet.

He Gives His Word

Ian Barclay

The Bible is the essential basis for Christian belief: it is particularly important to evangelicals. Too many take it for granted, however, and Ian Barclay challenges common assumptions held, and explains what the Bible is all about: its relevance, authorship, interpretations and apparent contradictions. He demonstrates the continuing centrality of the Bible and the fact that it still speaks directly to Christians today.